It's Me, WINDY Weather, Outside!

Brenda E. Thomas
Author and Illustrator

This book belongs to:

_____

✓   I promise to read this book.

✓   I promise to buddy read with my B.B.F.F,

✓   The Best book, ever!

It's Me, Windy Weather, Outside!

iUniverse books may be ordered through booksellers or by contacting:

iUniverse
1663 Liberty Drive
Bloomington, IN 47403
www.iuniverse.com
1-800-Authors (1-800-288-4677)

ISBN: 978-1-5320-4914-9 (sc)
ISBN: 978-1-5320-5000-8 (e)

Library of Congress Control Number: 2018905896

Print information available on the last page.

iUniverse rev. date: 06/07/2018

In Loving memory of my daughter
Te'Neil Nicole Thomas

"Do It Yourself, Mommy!"

Hello, It's me, Windy Weather Bear. I am a weather bear. I love everything about the weather and the seasons and the fun things that they can bring.

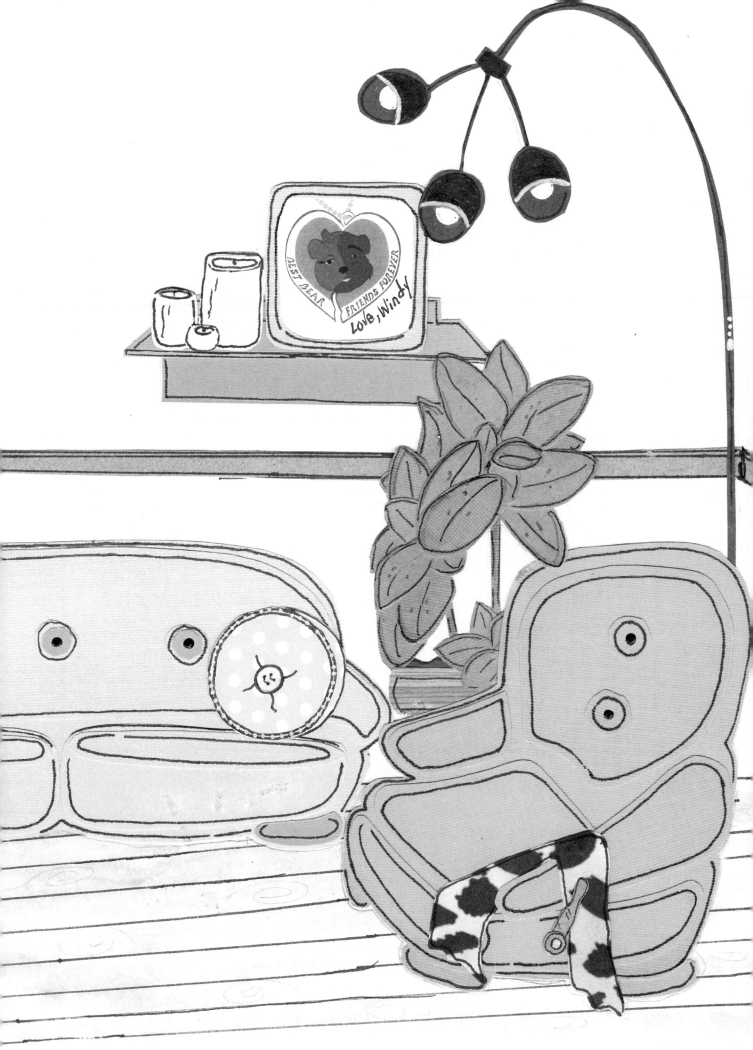

This is my B.B.F.F., Willie Weather Bear. I have lots of good friends, but Willie and I are Best Bear Friends, Forever! Do you have a best bear friend? A friend like Willie Weather Bear. I love, Willie! And this is my dog Tiny, my other good friend. He likes to go outside and play with me.

What do you like to do on a "Windy" day? Perhaps, you like to paint a picture, read a book, or like Willie ride a bike. As for me, I like to fly my kite. I am going outside to fly my kite. What will I need?

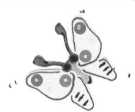

I will need to find my kite? Can you help me find my kite? Look! Here is my kite by the door.

I will need to find some string to help me pull my kite. Can you help me find some string? Look! Here is some string in my toy box.

I will need to find my kite's
tail. A tail will really help my kite to
sail. 1, 2, 3, … Can you look with me?
Look! Found it!

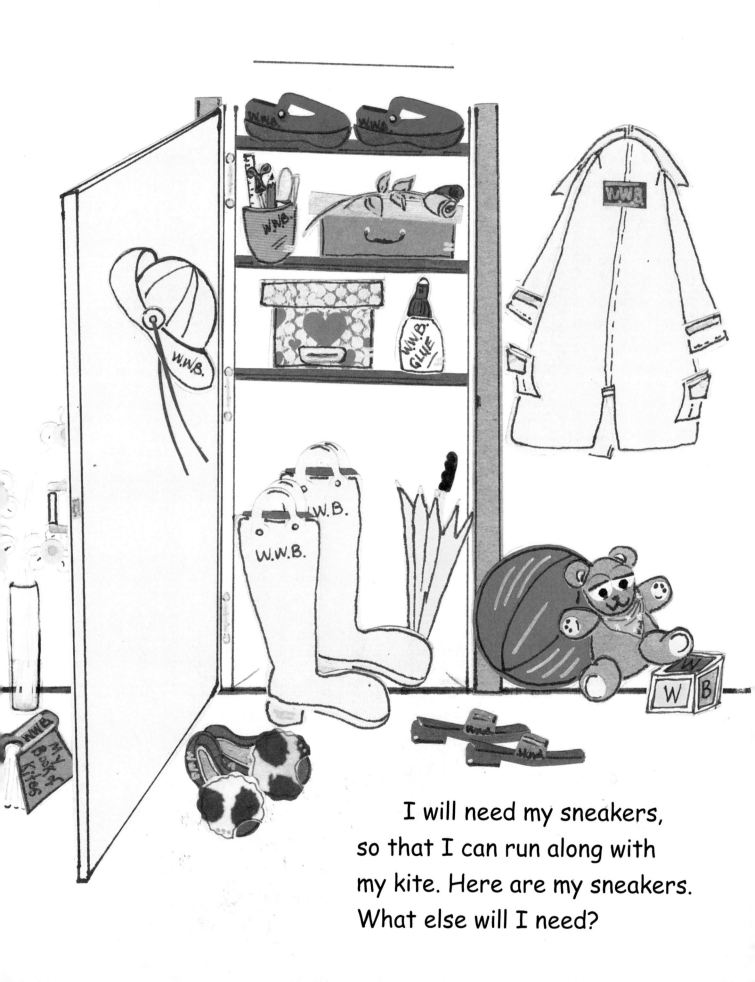

I will need my sneakers,
so that I can run along with
my kite. Here are my sneakers.
What else will I need?

I will need the wind to blow my kite. So, I will watch the trees to see which way the wind will blow. I will watch the leaves move that will also, let me know.

How does the wind know how to make my kite fly? Sometimes, the wind is breezy, and it blows, lightly.

Blow wind, Blow!

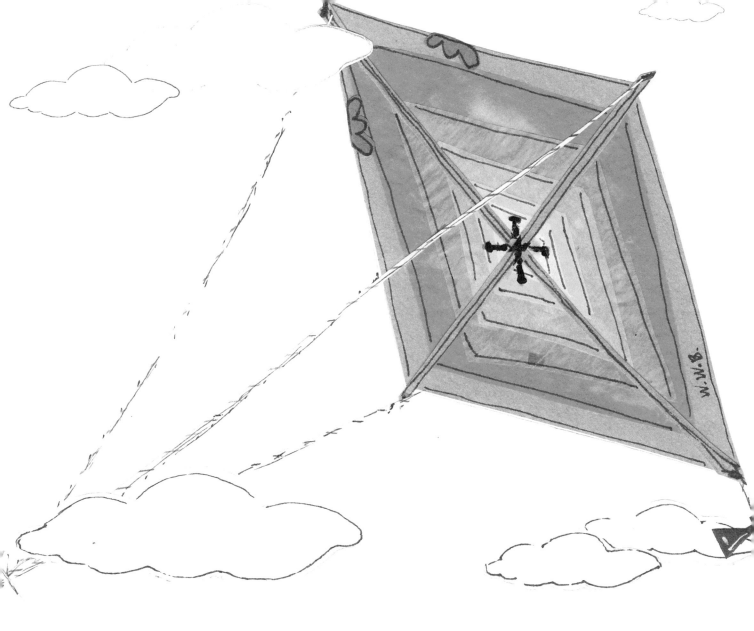

Sometimes, there is a gust of wind that blows my kite, mightily. The wind pushes my kite and gives it flight and then the wind blows my kite out of sight.

"Go Kite, Go!"

I will watch my kite as it goes higher and higher into the sky. Do you see how high my kite can go?

"LOOK!

My kite gets help from me... Windy! "It's Me, Windy Weather Outside!"

Windy's Kite First Flight Poem

It's Me, Windy Weather Bear.

Come outside with me, if you dare!

I am going outside to fly, fly, fly my kite.

My kite's first flight will be out, out, out of sight.

My kite's colors are beautiful hues, brilliant and bright.

Up, up, up in the air it goes, swirling through the sky.

It makes me run, run, run on my tiptoes.

My kite's string is long, tight and winding.

The tail is balanced, bowed and binding.

My kite goes through the air swirling

and twirling in the sky.

The wind blows, blows, blows my kite way up high!

Through the leaves, above the trees, and

over the clouds. Can you see?

My kite will fly with ease in the breeze

and I will play, play, play all day.

Because, my kite's first flight will be

way, way, way out of sight.

What makes my kite fly?

Gravity, Lift, Thrust and Drag are needed to make a kite fly. The string stops the kite from flying away as you hold it. The kite moves, backwards the wind is the power the kite needs to fly. Some kites need a lot of wind and some kites need very little wind to fly.

Gravity, Lift, Thrust and Drag are forces of nature that also assist the kite's movement. Gravity is the force that pulls the kite back down towards the ground. Lift stops the kite from falling, while pushing the kite up into the air. The force that helps the kite to move forward is called, thrust. Thrust, together with the tail helps the kite move from side to side and up and down. And, the Drag keeps the kite from moving, far to the left or to the right. The Drag works with the tail to keep good balance. The tail should not be too long or too short. If the tail is to heavy the kite will not be balanced, it will just spin around and around.

Gravity – pulls down.
Lift – stops the pull down.
Thrust – forces movement.
Drag- keeps the centers balance
The Tail – balances

Printed in the United States
By Bookmasters